POWERFUL MILITARY AIRCRAFT

CYNTHIA KENNEDY HENZEL

childsworld.com

Published by The Child's World®
800-599-READ • www.childsworld.com

Photography Credits
Photographs ©: Master Sgt. Jeremy Lock/Defense Media Activity/US Air Force/DVIDS, cover, 1; Tech. Sgt. Matthew Plew/US Air Force, 3; Capt. Robert Taylor/Idaho Army National Guard/DVIDS, 5; Capt. Edward Benedictus/101st Combat Aviation Brigade/DVIDS, 6; 1st Lt. Savanah Bray/53rd Wing/US Air Force/DVIDS, 9, 16 (F-15EX); Staff Sgt. Bennie J. Davis III/US Air Force, 11; Cpl. Ken Kalemkarian/Marine Corps Air Station Yuma/DVIDS, 12; Lance Cpl. Kerstin Roberts/Marine Corps Base Camp Pendleton/US Marine Corps/DVIDS, 15; Tech. Sgt. Miguel Lara/509th Bomb Wing Public Affairs/US Air Force/DVIDS, 16 (B-2); Nicholas Pilch/60th Air Mobility Wing Public Affairs/US Air Force/DVIDS, 16 (C-5M); Master Sgt. John Nimmo, Sr./4th Combat Camera Squadron/US Air Force/DVIDS, 16 (F-35); Staff Sgt. Mary McKnight/916th Air Refueling Wing/US Air Force/DVIDS, 16 (KC-46A); Staff Sgt. Robert Trujillo/9th Reconnaissance Wing Public Affairs/US Air Force/DVIDS, 16 (U-2); Sgt. Emily Finn/35th Combat Aviation Brigade/US Army National Guard/DVIDS, 19; Sgt. Henry Villarama/173rd Airborne Brigade/US Army/DVIDS, 20

ISBN Information
9781503816695 (Reinforced Library Binding)
9781503881372 (Portable Document Format)
9781503882683 (Online Multi-user eBook)
9781503883994 (Electronic Publication)

LCCN 2022951182

Printed in the United States of America

ABOUT THE AUTHOR

Cynthia Kennedy Henzel has a BS in social studies education and an MS in geography. She has worked as a teacher-educator in many countries. Currently, she writes fiction and nonfiction books and develops education materials for social studies, history, science, and ELL students. She has written more than 100 books and 150 stories for young people.

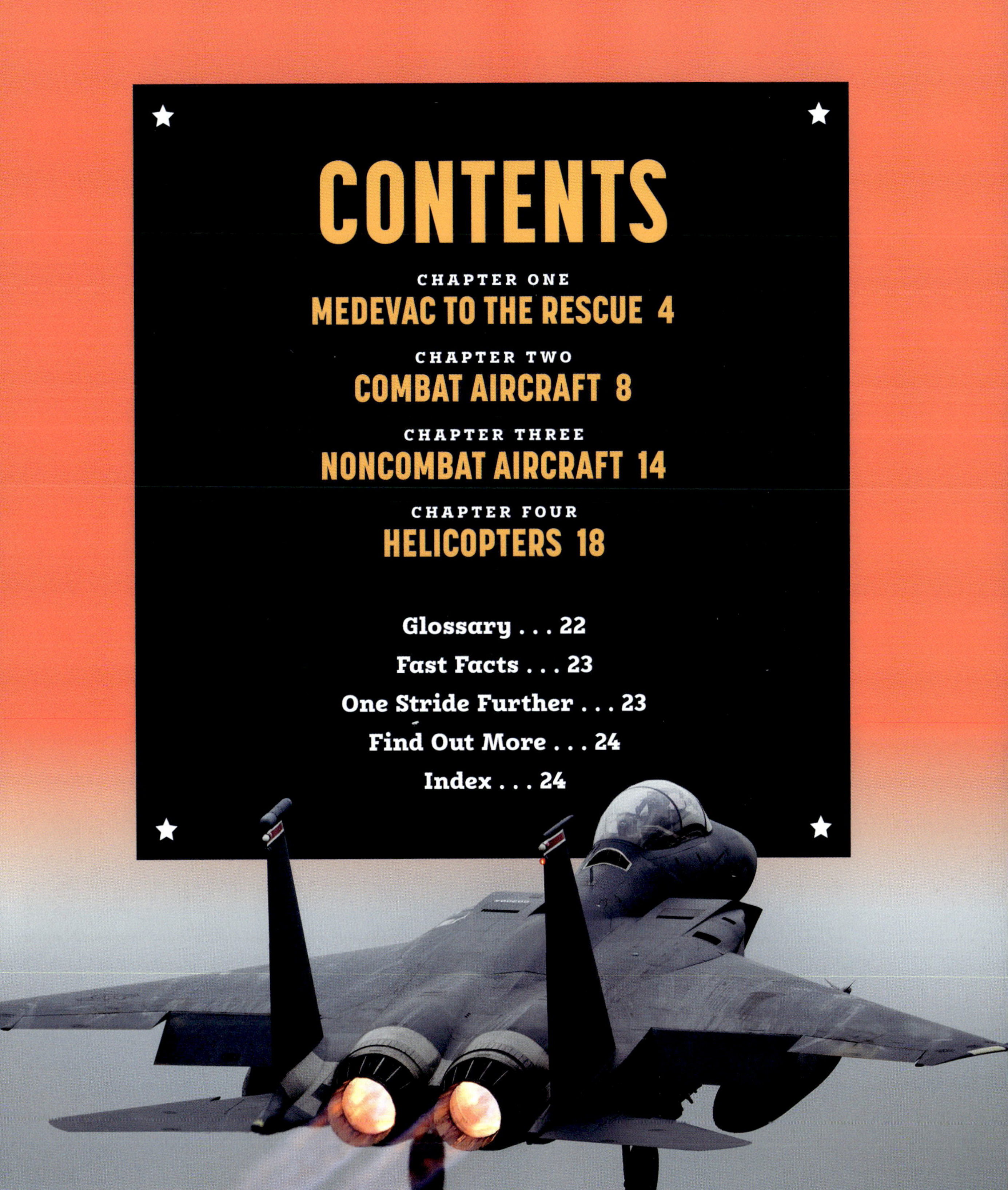

CONTENTS

CHAPTER ONE

MEDEVAC TO THE RESCUE

The lieutenant sees a red cross on the door of the Black Hawk helicopter. "Thank goodness," he thinks. It is the medical **evacuation** (medevac) helicopter. The lieutenant has two wounded soldiers. They need medical care immediately.

A storm is moving in. But the helicopter has a powerful engine and **rotor** system. These features allow the Black Hawk to carry heavy loads even in bad weather.

The **terrain** is too rough for the helicopter to land. But it doesn't need to. The Black Hawk slowly descends and then **hovers** nearby. The blades are blowing sand everywhere. The noise is deafening. The lieutenant sees a basket lowered from the helicopter. It looks like a hospital stretcher. This rescue basket is called a litter. The Black Hawk uses a system of **thrusters** on the corners of the litter to keep it steady. Small blasts of air keep the litter from swinging or turning.

Soldiers practice the medical evacuation process. This helps real evacuations go smoothly.

Medical teams practice raising the litter and loading it into the helicopter with a life-size model strapped in.

The soldiers place one soldier on the litter. It slowly rises. The helicopter crew guides it aboard. Moments later, the litter comes back down. The second wounded soldier is lifted into the Black Hawk.

"You need to go, too," says the lieutenant's next-in-command.

The lieutenant looks where she is pointing. He had not noticed the wound in his arm. He nods before ducking low and running to the waiting litter. The medevac crew pulls him aboard.

It's a hot day, but it is cool inside the helicopter. The sealed windows keep out the heat. The other wounded soldiers are already hooked up to patient **monitors**. One is wearing an oxygen mask. The Black Hawk medevac is like a flying ambulance. It has medical equipment to care for wounded soldiers.

Everything is under control. The lieutenant's arm hurts badly. But the high-tech medevac helicopter and crew have saved his soldiers' lives.

The Black Hawk medevac is a specially designed helicopter used to evacuate the wounded. It is just one of the high-tech aircraft operated by the US military. Some aircraft specialize in moving cargo. Some specialize in guarding the US coasts. Combat aircraft are designed to stay hidden from enemies while fighting from the sky. Together, these powerful aircraft are important in battle and in keeping the United States safe.

CHAPTER TWO

COMBAT AIRCRAFT

Combat aircraft include fighters and bombers. Fighters are used to scare off or destroy enemy aircraft. They are small and fast. They can quickly turn, dive, and roll as they fight. Fighter jets carry missiles that they can shoot at enemy targets. These aircraft also carry machine guns. They can fire these guns at enemies in the sky or on the ground.

One important US fighter jet is the F-15. The F-15EX Eagle II is a high-tech version of this aircraft. It has advanced weapons and technology. For example, it can carry hypersonic weapons. Hypersonic missiles can travel five times the speed of sound. That's more than 3,800 miles per hour (6,120 kmh). These missiles are some of the fastest in the world. The F-15EX Eagle II is the first US fighter jet designed to carry these weapons.

The first F-15EX Eagle II was added to the US Air Force in March 2021.

OT
53 WG
002

Bombers attack targets on the ground by dropping bombs. These aircraft are designed to carry thousands of pounds of explosives. But bombers usually do not have weapons to fight other planes.

Some combat aircraft use **stealth** technology. These aircraft stay hidden from **radar**. Radar works by sending out radio signals. Those signals bounce off nearby objects. Radar equipment detects the reflections of the signals. It can then tell where those objects are. Stealth aircraft are designed so radar can't find them. Their shapes reflect the signals in different directions instead of back to the radar equipment. Special coatings on stealth aircraft can absorb some radar signals, too.

The B-2 Spirit is one of the US military's most important stealth bombers. The B-2 is often one of the first aircraft into battle. Its famous design looks like a flying black wing. This shape helps keep the B-2 invisible to enemies. It can fly long distances and refuel in midair. The B-2 can reach any point in the world within hours. It can carry 40,000 pounds (18,140 kg) of bombs.

The B-2 Spirit is 172 feet (52 m) across and only 17 feet (5 m) tall. This shape helps with its stealth.

The F-35 Lightning II is a Short Take-Off and Vertical Landing (STOVL) aircraft. It can take off from a very short runway, and it can come straight down to land.

The F-22 Raptor fighter is almost invisible to radar. It is used for **reconnaissance**, attack, and electronic warfare. Electronic warfare includes jamming enemy radio signals or interfering with equipment operation. The US military has not shared the Raptor's technology with any other country.

The F-35 Lightning II fighter can attack both air and ground targets. It is one of the deadliest planes in the US military. The Marines use a version called the F-35B. This airplane can take off like a helicopter. Its engines point downward to push the F-35 into the air. Then the engines rotate backward so the plane can fly normally.

BLUE ANGELS

The Blue Angels is a group of 17 Navy and Marine pilots who put on air shows for the public. They do difficult aircraft maneuvers such as the Diamond Roll, in which four jets roll together while flying at 400 miles per hour (640 kmh). In the Diamond 360, four jets fly together. There are only 18 inches (46 cm) between the tip of one plane's wing and the **cockpit** of another. The Blue Angels formed in 1946 to demonstrate the teamwork and professionalism of the US Navy and Marine Corps.

CHAPTER THREE

NONCOMBAT AIRCRAFT

The military uses aircraft for more than just combat. Noncombat aircraft provide the military with what they need when they need it. These aircraft move troops and supplies. Noncombat aircraft are also used for reconnaissance. They can patrol US coasts and gather information about enemies.

The C-5M Super Galaxy is the largest US military aircraft. It is longer than five school buses and as tall as a five-story building. It has four engines and 28 wheels. The Super Galaxy can carry a load weighing 281,000 pounds (127,460 kg) for more than 2,000 miles (3,220 km) without refueling. This load could include two Abrams battle tanks or 16 Humvee trucks.

Air tankers are responsible for carrying fuel. The KC-46A Pegasus is a multipurpose aircraft. It is a tanker capable of carrying 212,300 pounds (96,300 kg) of fuel.

The nose of the C-5M Super Galaxy opens for troops to unload cargo. The doors at the back of the aircraft can open, too.

AIR MOBILITY COMMAND

PLANE WINGSPAN

F-15EX Eagle II:
43 feet (13 m)

C-5M Super Galaxy:
223 feet (68 m)

F-35 Lightning II:
35 feet (11 m)

B-2 Spirit:
172 feet (52 m)

KC-46A Pegasus:
156 feet (47.5 m)

U-2 Dragon Lady:
105 feet (32 m)

The Pegasus is also used for medical evacuations. It has 15 seats for the air crew, including seats for five medical professionals.

The Pegasus can fuel another aircraft while both aircraft are flying. First, the other aircraft approaches the Pegasus within 100 feet (30 m). Next, a Pegasus crew member directs a pipe called a boom from the tanker into a small opening on the other aircraft. As the two aircraft fly together, the fuel is transferred at 6,000 pounds (2,722 kg) per minute. Once the refueling is done, the boom is disconnected.

Noncombat aircraft are used by multiple branches of the US military. The Navy flies reconnaissance aircraft such as the E-2 Hawkeye. The Hawkeye carries a giant radar antenna and protective dome on its back. Its job is to monitor US airspace for threats. The Hawkeye's crew members communicate with other pilots in the area. The crew members tell other pilots where they are needed.

THE U-2

One unique reconnaissance aircraft is the U-2 Dragon Lady. The U-2 is long and narrow. It is light enough that it does not need to refuel midflight. It flies more than 70,000 feet (21,300 m) above the ground. This is so high in the sky that it is almost in space. Pilots wear suits like those that astronauts wear.

A plane's wingspan is measured from the tip of one wing to the tip of the other. Different sizes of aircraft are used for different purposes.

CHAPTER FOUR

HELICOPTERS

Helicopters are important military aircraft because they can land and take off where planes cannot. Helicopters have a spinning rotor on top of the aircraft. This allows the aircraft to take off straight up into the air. They don't need a runway like a plane. They can hover over one point, too. Helicopters can fly low over the ground. Military helicopters have armor and special windshields to protect the aircraft and its passengers. In small spaces or rough terrain, helicopters can save the day.

The most common military helicopter is the UH-60 Black Hawk. It is a multipurpose aircraft. It can attack enemies or transport troops. The Black Hawk is also used for search-and-rescue missions. It can carry 11 people.

Some soldiers learn to climb down from a hovering helicopter. This allows troops to access places where the helicopter cannot land.

UNITED STATES ARMY

194

One very powerful attack helicopter is the AH-1Z Viper. It can attack other aircraft as well as ground targets. The Viper can protect troops and cargo from above. In the cockpit, the pilot sits behind the copilot. The copilot controls the weapons.

Transport helicopters deliver or pick up troops and cargo. The CH-47 Chinook is one of the largest transport helicopters in the US military. It has one rotor at the front and one at the back. It is powerful enough to carry 33 soldiers and all their gear. The Chinook is commonly used to move supplies or people during natural disasters. The US military has depended on the Chinook for more than 60 years.

Many US military aircraft have served for decades. But the military also continues to invent and build new technology to protect the country. Today's combat aircraft are stronger and stealthier than in the past. Noncombat aircraft keep the military running smoothly and the coasts safe. Each aircraft plays an important part in the US military.

When cargo is too large to fit inside the Chinook, it can be hung from wires below the helicopter.

GLOSSARY

cockpit (KOK-pit) The cockpit is the part of the aircraft where the pilot sits. The fighter jet's cockpit had room for only one person.

evacuation (ih-vak-yoo-AY-shun) Evacuation means to move people away from danger. The helicopter evacuation moved wounded soldiers away from the battlefield.

hovers (HUH-vers) When something hovers, it stays in one spot in the air. A helicopter hovers over the battlefield.

monitors (MAA-nuh-tuhrs) Medical monitors show information about a patient's health. Monitors tracked the patient's heart rate.

radar (RAY-dar) Radar is an equipment system that sends out signals and then detects the reflections of those signals after they bounce off objects. Aircraft use radar to track enemies.

reconnaissance (reh-KON-nuh-sens) Reconnaissance is looking over an area to locate important features and information. The aircraft did reconnaissance of enemy territory by flying overhead.

rotor (ROH-tur) A rotor is a mechanical part that spins. The helicopter has a rotor with blades on it that allows the aircraft to fly.

stealth (STELTH) Stealth means an object was made difficult to detect. The aircraft used stealth technology to avoid radar detection.

terrain (tuh-RAYN) Terrain means an area of land and its natural features. The helicopter was able to land on the rough terrain.

thrusters (THRUH-sters) Thrusters are engines or devices that blow a strong blast of air to control direction or speed. The litter's thrusters kept it stable.

FAST FACTS

- Medevac aircraft fly wounded people off the battlefield. Doctors and nurses can treat soldiers' wounds in the aircraft.
- Fighter jets such as the F-15EX Eagle II, F-22 Raptor, and F-35 Lightning II fight enemies in the air.
- Bombers such as the B-2 Spirit carry heavy loads of bombs to drop.
- Naval aircraft such as the E-2 Hawkeye use radar to look out for enemies.
- Cargo aircraft move troops and supplies to where they are needed. The largest cargo aircraft in the US military is the C-5M Super Galaxy.
- Helicopters can land on rough terrain and hover over the ground.
- The US military's most-used helicopter is the Black Hawk.

ONE STRIDE FURTHER

- Stealth technology is important to keep aircraft safe. For what kind of missions do you think stealth aircraft are most useful?
- What advantages do helicopters have over airplanes? What advantages do airplanes have? Think of a situation in which it is better to have one or the other.
- Imagine you are a pilot. Which type of aircraft would you prefer to fly? Explain your choice.

FIND OUT MORE

IN THE LIBRARY

Brody, Walt. *How Military Helicopters Work.* Minneapolis, MN: Lerner Publications, 2020.

Oxlade, Chris. *Inside Fighter Planes.* Minneapolis, MN: Hungry Tomato, 2018.

Ringstad, Arnold. *Powerful Missiles and Bombs.* Parker, CO: The Child's World, 2024.

ON THE WEB

Visit our website for links about military aircraft:
childsworld.com/links

Note to Parents, Caregivers, Teachers, and Librarians: We routinely verify our Web links to make sure they are safe and active sites. So encourage your readers to check them out!

INDEX